TOP TRADE
CAREERS

LEGAL ASSISTANT

A Crabtree Branches Book

Kelli Hicks

CRABTREE
Publishing Company
www.crabtreebooks.com

School-to-Home Support for Caregivers and Teachers

This high-interest book is designed to motivate striving students with engaging topics while building fluency, vocabulary, and an interest in reading. Here are a few questions and activities to help the reader build upon his or her comprehension skills.

Before Reading:

- *What do I think this book is about?*
- *What do I know about this topic?*
- *What do I want to learn about this topic?*
- *Why am I reading this book?*

During Reading:

- *I wonder why...*
- *I'm curious to know...*
- *How is this like something I already know?*
- *What have I learned so far?*

After Reading:

- *What was the author trying to teach me?*
- *What are some details?*
- *How did the photographs and captions help me understand more?*
- *Read the book again and look for the vocabulary words.*
- *What questions do I still have?*

Extension Activities:

- *What was your favorite part of the book? Write a paragraph on it.*
- *Draw a picture of your favorite thing you learned from the book.*

TABLE OF CONTENTS

It's the Law 4

A Legal Team 6

Where Do I Start? 10

Special Skills 12

What a Challenge! 22

How Much Do I Make? 24

Making a Difference 26

Glossary 30

Index 31

Websites to Visit 31

About the Author 32

IT'S THE LAW

A lawyer, also known as an attorney, is an expert on the law. A lawyer helps people to know their legal rights.

Lawyers write persuasive arguments based on the law. They will sometimes appear in court to support their **clients**.

A LEGAL TEAM

Lawyers cannot do all this work on their own. Lawyers rely on legal assistants for help.

A legal assistant has knowledge of the law and works with the lawyer to help **research**, organize, and communicate with clients.

Are paralegals and legal assistants the same? Both jobs include similar tasks. Paralegals usually have more education and they may also bill their working hours differently than legal assistants.

Many **law firms** rely on legal assistants to help handle their heavy caseloads. Most legal assistants work in a law office.

They do their job with the guidance of a lawyer. Legal assistants may accompany the lawyer to hearings in court.

Besides legal assistants, many law firms have other members on their team. A legal secretary works in the law office and schedules appointments, maintains records, and keeps track of documents.

If you want to be a legal assistant, you must have a high school diploma. Most law firms require that legal assistants have the diploma or **degree** required for the job. In many places, legal assistants are also required to take a test to earn their **certification**.

Some law firms prefer that legal assistants have a four-year degree called a Bachelor's degree.

Some nurses add to their nursing degree. They study to become a certified paralegal, too. They specialize in working with insurance claims, personal injury cases, and medical lawsuits. They use their legal knowledge to help doctors and nurses understand the laws concerning medicine.

SPECIAL SKILLS

Do you think you have the skills to be a legal assistant? First, you need to be a great communicator. Using the right words to talk with clients and relaying information to the lawyers **accurately** is important.

You should have strong computer skills and be able to create documents and track information in an organized way on the computer.

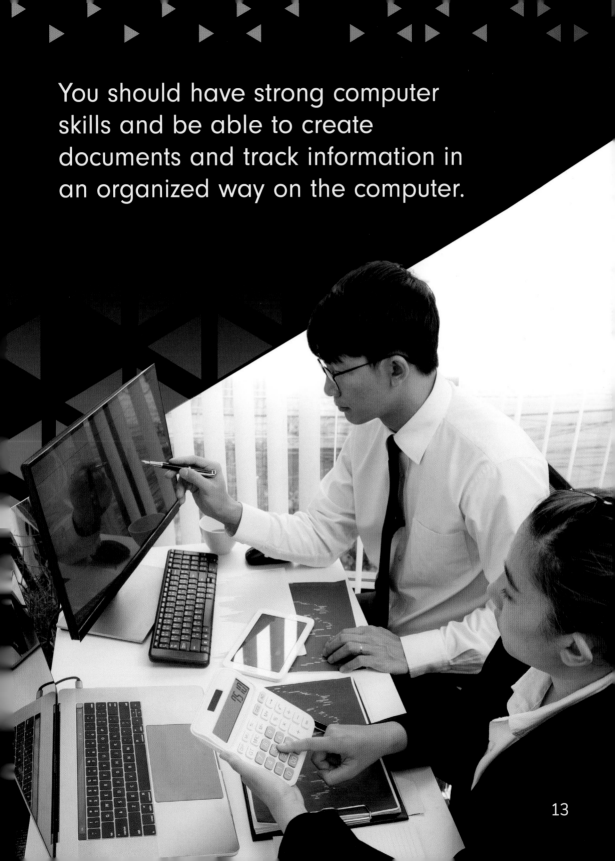

Legal assistants often help with researching information. They might find old cases or past **judgments** that can help with the current case.

Legal assistants are skilled writers and work on producing contracts. Legal assistants can write the documents, but the lawyer has to provide the official signature.

Are you focused and able to pay attention to the little details? These are necessary abilities for being a legal assistant.

Every day is different, so you have to be able to **adapt** easily and be flexible. You need to stay calm and have patience.

There are many benefits to being a legal assistant. You can get a degree relatively quickly without spending too much money.

Legal assistants are in demand and there are many jobs available.

Besides working for a law firm, many businesses also need legal assistants. You may find work in entertainment, sports, marketing, medicine, or many other fields.

Big law firms may have many legal assistants to handle the large number of cases. A paralegal manager organizes the team of legal assistants and helps manage the daily tasks that arise. The manager must be certified and have at least five years of experience.

Although many legal assistants work for a law firm or a lawyer, some are **self-employed**. They may provide services to many different clients and maintain a flexible schedule.

WHAT A CHALLENGE!

There are some challenges in this career. Legal assistants often have to work long hours to meet tight **deadlines**.

Evening or weekend hours might be required when preparing for a trial. This can be stressful! Legal assistants also have to be able to juggle multiple tasks or cases at one time.

HOW MUCH DO I MAKE?

Becoming a legal assistant can be a rewarding career. Not only can you help people, but you can earn a good living as well.

Your salary may be affected by where you live, your level of experience, and whether you work for someone else or for yourself.

Legal Assistant	$31,000 - $70,000
Paralegal	$31,000 - $71,000
Legal Secretary	$30,000 - $80,000
Corporate Paralegal	$46,000 - $94,000
Paralegal Manager	$88,573 - $119,654
Nurse Paralegal	$70,600 - $90,220

MAKING A DIFFERENCE

Legal assistants are important workers. They can help to prove a person's innocence, or help make sure that the rights of an individual are respected.

They can assist people in resolving their differences, and make sure the law is followed. A legal assistant uses knowledge of the law to stand up for others who need help.

Merrell Williams Jr. worked as a paralegal in a law firm in Kentucky. He provided evidence that tobacco was an addictive product and helped to win a $206 billion settlement against major tobacco companies for hiding the truth from the public.

All people need help from time to time and a legal assistant is a person who can positively influence the lives of others.

Legal assistants are valuable members of the community and can give a voice to people in need.

accurately (AK-yuh-ruht-lee): exactly correct

adapt (uh-DAPT): to change because of a new situation

certification (sur-tif-uh-KAY-shuhn): an official document to prove an achievement or status

clients (KLYE-uhntz): people who use the services of a professional person

deadlines (DED-lines): a time by which a piece of work or job must be finished

degree (di-GREE): a title given by a college or university for completing coursework

judgments (JUHJ-muhntz): decisions made by a judge

law firms (law furmz): businesses or companies that practice law

research (REE-surch): to study and find out about a subject

self-employed (self-EM-ployd): you work for yourself, not an employer; you are your own boss

INDEX

arguments 5

career 24

clients 5, 7, 12, 21

court 5, 8

contracts 15

diploma/degree 10

knowledge 7, 27

law 4, 5, 7, 11, 27

paralegal 7, 11, 20

salary 25

skill(s) 12, 13

WEBSITES TO VISIT

www.thebalancecareers.com/the-8-best-things-about-being-a-paralegal-2164597

https://kids.kiddle.co/Paralegal

www.americanbar.org/groups/paralegals/profession-information/educational-information-for-paralegals

ABOUT THE AUTHOR

Kelli Hicks

Kelli Hicks is teacher and writer who lives with her family in Florida. She loves to watch shows about true crime and the courts. She tries her best to follow the law and be a good citizen.

CRABTREE
Publishing Company

Written by: Kelli Hicks
Designed by: Jennifer Dydyk
Edited by: Tracy Nelson Maurer
Proofreader: Ellen Rodger
Print and production coordinator:
Katherine Berti

Photographs: Cover career logo icon © Trueffelpix, diamond pattern used on cover and throughout book © Aleksandr Andrushkiv, cover photo © Prostock-studio, photo of legal document on cover and title page © Mameraman, Page 4 © Elnur, page 5 top photo © GaudiLab, bottom photo © wavebreakmedia, Page 6 © Blue Planet Studio, Page 7 © Shine Nucha, Page 8 © wavebreakmedia, Page 9 top photo © Evok20, bottom photo © monte_a, Page 10 Matt Benoit, Page 11 top photo © ALPA PROD, bottom photo © Rawpixel.com, Page 12 top photo © fizkes, bottom photo © Golubovy, Page 13 © ZozerEblola, Page 14 top photo © jjphotos, bottom photo © fizkes, Page 15 © smolaw, Page 16 © Syda Productions, Page 17 top photo © fizkes, bottom photo © insta_photos, Page 18 photo © Tatiana Frank, illustrations pages 18 and 19 © Edge Creative, Page 19 photo © fizkes, Page 20 illustrations © Martin Kalimon, photo © adriaticfoto, Page 21 © krakenimages.com, Page 22 top photo © Motortion Films, bottom photo © smolaw, Page 23 © DC Studio, Page 24 © Vitalii Stock, Page 25 © ALPA PROD, Page 26 © ESB Professional, Page 27 top photo © Atstock Productions, bottom photo © Thichaa, Page 28 © Elnur, Page 29 © El Nariz. All images from Shutterstock.com

Library and Archives Canada Cataloguing in Publication

Available at the Library and Archives Canada

Library of Congress Cataloging-in-Publication Data

Available at the Library of Congress

Crabtree Publishing Company

www.crabtreebooks.com   1-800-387-7650

Copyright © 2022 **CRABTREE PUBLISHING COMPANY**

Published in the United States
Crabtree Publishing
347 Fifth Avenue
Suite 1402-145
New York, NY, 10016

Published in Canada
Crabtree Publishing
616 Welland Ave.
St. Catharines, ON
L2M 5V6

Printed in the U.S.A./CG20210915/012022